DELAWARE PHARMACY LAW

Q & A

Table of Contents   Pages

PART ONE

PART-ONE

1. Who appoints the board members in Delaware?

   a. The governor

   b. The city counsels

   c. The Human resource department

   d. The supreme court

2. Who can counsel a patient or a patient's agent?

   I.   A pharmacy interns

   II. A pharmacist

   III. A pharmacy technician

   IV. The pharmacy owner

   a. I only

   b. III only

   c. I and II only

   d. II and III only

3. A pharmacy must retain prescriptions for at least:

   a. 1 year

   b. 2 years

   c. 3 years

   d. 4 years.

4. A pharmacist must administer an authorized vaccine using:

    I.   A prescription.

    II.   A protocol.

    III.   A standing order.

    a.   I only

    b.   III only

    c.   I and II

    d.   II and II

    e.   I, II and III

5. A pharmacist who wants to become a nuclear pharmacist must attain a minimum of_____ hours of training under the supervision of a nuclear pharmacist.

    a.   15000 hours

    b.   2000 hours

    c.   3000 hours

    d.   5000 hours

    e.   500 hours

6. Who is authorized to possess a key of a pharmacy?

    a.   The pharmacy owner

    b.   The front store manager

    c.   The lead technician

    d.   The pharmacist

7. In Delaware, pharmacy technicians are NOT required to be:

    I.   Registered.

    II.   Licensed.

    III.   Certified.

    a. I only

    b. III only

    c. I and

    d. I and II

    e. II and III

8. A pharmacist who wants to register as a nuclear pharmacist must have received a minimum of_____ contact hours of didactic instruction in nuclear pharmacy.

    a. 100 contact hours

    b. 200 contact hours

    c. 250 contact hours

    d. 500 contact hours

    e. 60 contact hours

9. A Non-resident pharmacy could be a pharmacy that ships prescription drugs into Delaware located.

    I.   In Hawaii

    II.   In New Jersey

    III.   In Haiti

    IV.   Peru

a. I only

b. III only

c. I and II only

d. II and III

10. What is the minimum age limit to buy insulin syringe in Delaware?

    a. 15 years

    b. 16 years

    c. 17 years

    d. 18 years

11. It is required if the purchaser wants more than 10 syringes at a time.

    a. Yes, the prescription is required.

    b. No, it is not required

12. What the monthly sale limit of pseudoephedrine without prescription in Delaware?

    a. 3.6 g

    b. 7.5 g

    c. 9 g

    d. 12 g

13. What shall be recorded on the back of a prescription for a schedule III drug upon partial fill?

    a. The patient's name.

    b. The date of prescription issued.

    c. The amount of drug dispensed if different from the amount written on the prescription

    d. The drug names.

14. What is the data collection interval under the prescription drug monitoring program?

    a. Within 36 hours of dispensing

    b. Within 48 hours of dispensing.

    c. Within 72 hours of dispensing.

    d. Within 24 hours of dispensing.

15. Who may perform drug utilization review?

    I. Pharmacist

    II. Lead technician

    III. Pharmacist intern

    IV. Pharmacy owner

    a. I only

    b. III only

    c. I and I only

    d. I and III only

16. If a pharmacy is going to be closed for more than seven consecutive business days, the Board must be notified:

    a. 10 days prior to the temporary closing.

    b. 14 days prior to the temporary closing.

    c. 3 days prior to the temporary closing.

    d. 5 days prior to the temporary closing.

17. For a pharmacist, at least how many hours of continuing education per biennial licensure period must be in the area of medication safety/errors?

    a. At least 4 hours

    b. At least 3 hours

    c. At least 1 hour

    d. At least 2 hours

18. The Delaware board of pharmacy:

    I. Requires oral counselling in certain situations or an "offer to counsel"

    II. Requires documentation of patient's refusal for counselling.

    III. Require to counsel new prescriptions and refills.

    a. I only

    b. III only

    c. I and II

    d. II and III

    e. I, II and III

9

19. Records related to an Automated Pharmacy System shall be kept for a period of:

    a. 2 years.

    b. 3 years.

    c. 4 years.

    d. 5 years.

20. A maximum of how many times a refill prescription can be transferred between pharmacies sharing a real-time on-line database for a schedule III drug prescription with five refills on it?

    a. Five refills

    b. Eleven refills

    c. one refills

    d. Six refills

    e. None

21. What is the maximum amount of pseudoephedrine base that may be purchased in 1 day?

    a. 2.4 g

    b. 3.6 g

    c. 9 g

    d. 10 g

22. If a drug has no accepted medical use and extremely high potential for abuse, which DEA schedule would it be categorized in?

    a. Schedule I.

    b. Schedule II.

    c. Schedule III.

    d. Schedule IV.

23. How much time does a physician have to provide a written prescription for an "emergency prescription" for a Schedule II drug?

    a. 24 hours

    b. 48 hours

    c. 72 hours

    d. 7 days

24. Which of the following pieces of information is not required on a prescription label?

    a. Directions for use

    b. Name and address of the pharmacy

    c. Name and address of the prescriber

    d. Telephone number of the prescriber

25. How many times may a prescription with "prn" refills be transferred from a pharmacy

    a. 0 times

    b. 1 time

    c. 5 times

    d. 6 times

26. In what schedule is acetaminophen with codeine placed?

    a. II

    b. III

    c. IV

    d. V

27. How many refills are allowed on C-IV drugs?

    a. 5

    b. 3

    c. 1

    d. 0

28. Which schedule has no medicinal use?

    a. Schedule I

    b. Schedule II

    c. Schedule III

    d. Schedule IV

29. What is the schedule for 1.8 grams of codeine in a 100 ml solution?

    a.   Schedule II

    b.   Schedule III

    c.   Schedule IV

    d.   Schedule V

30. Per Federal laws, how long does the pharmacy keep records of schedule II drugs?

    a.   2 years

    b.   3 years

    c.   5 years

    d.   7 years

31. Long-term detoxification treatment should not be longer than:

    a.   30 days

    b.   60 days

    c.   120 days

    d.   180 days

32. Per Federal laws, in order to buy pseudoephedrine related OTC Schedule V drugs, the purchaser should be at least _____ old.

    a. 16 years

    b. 18 years

    c. 21 years

    d. 23 years

33. What are the total days of supply of Simvastatin 20 mg prescription that may be dispensed with authorized refills, as long as it doesn't exceed the total quantity authorized by the prescriber?

    a. 30 days

    b. 60 days

    c. 90 days

    d. 120 days

34. Per Federal law what is the quantity limit of schedule II drugs to be dispensed at a time?

    a. 30 days

    b. 60 days

    c. 90 days

    d. 120 days

35. What is the schedule for 500 mg of opium in a 100 ml solution?

    a. Schedule II

    b. Schedule III

    c. Schedule IV

    d. Schedule V

36. Records of pseudoephedrine sales shall be maintained by the pharmacy for:

    a. At least 6 months

    b. At least 1 year

    c. At least 2 years.

    d. At least 3 years

37. If a computerized system is used to maintain prescription records, it shall be designed so that the pharmacy can receive a printout of any refill data_____ days after requesting the printout.

    a. 2 days

    b. 3 days

    c. 4 days

    d. 5 days

38. Schedule II controlled substances can be:

    I.   Stored in a securely locked cabinet.

    II.   Dispersed throughout the inventory of non-controlled substances.

    III.   Kept separate from all other drugs.

    a. I only

    b. II only

    c. III only

    d. I, II and III only

39. Immunization prescriptions must be maintained for at least

    a. 1 year.

    b. 2 years.

    c. 3 years.

    d. 4 years.

40. A pharmacist can administer all of the following vaccine except:

    a. Shingles vaccines.

    b. Influenza vaccines.

    c. Meningitis vaccines.

    d. Pneumonia vaccines.

    e. None of the above.

41. A schedules II prescription will become void unless dispensed within _____ days of the original date of the prescription.

    a.   5 days

    b.   7 days

    c.   10 days

    d.   30 days

42. In Delaware, pharmacist licenses expire on:

    a.   May 31 of odd years.

    b.   October 30 of even years.

    c.   July 31 of even years.

    d.   September 30 of even years.

43. Who can sell a product containing pseudoephedrine without a prescription?

    I.   A pharmacy interns.

    II.   A pharmacy technician.

    III.   A pharmacy clerks.

    a.   I only

    b.   III only

    c.   I and I

    d.   II and Ill

    e.   I, II and III

44. How many hours of CEs are required to collect by a

pharmacist per renewal period in Delaware?

    a. 10 hours

    b. 20 hours

    c. 30 hours

    d. 40 hours

45. Under the Delaware Pharmacy Law, prescriptions for Schedule
II controlled substances cannot be written nor dispensed for
more than:

    a. 100 dosage units.

    b. 120 dosage units.

    c. 180 dosage units

    d. 210 dosage units

46. Under the Delaware Pharmacy Law, prescriptions for Schedule

II controlled substances cannot be written nor dispensed for

more than _____ days.

    a. 14 days

    b. 31 days

    c. 90 days

    d. 180 days

47. Licensed pharmacy shall notify the Delaware board of the intended closing _____ days before a licensed pharmacy closes or ceases the operation.

    a. At least 10 days

    b. At least 14 days

    c. At least 21 days

    d. At least 28 days

48. The partial filling of a schedule II drugs for terminally ill patients must be carried out within:

    a. 10 days from the initial filling

    b. 96 hours from the initial filling.

    c. 30 days from the initial filling.

    d. 72 hours from the initial filling

49. Who can NOT possess controlled substances in Delaware?

    I. Optometrists
    II. Dentists
    III. Nurse Midwives
    IV. Physician assistant

    a. I only

    b. III only

    c. I and II

    d. II and I

    e. I, II and III

50. How many hours of practical experience are required by an intern?

    a. At least 1200 hours

    b. At least 1300 hours

    c. At least 1800 hours

    d. At least 1500 hours

51. An authorized prescriber must mail a copy of an emergency oral prescription for a schedule II drug within_____ after an oral authorization.

    a. 72 hours

    b. 7 days

    c. 14 days

    d. 30 days

52. In Delaware, the Board of Pharmacy consists of how many board members?

    a. 6

    b. 7

    c. 8

    d. 9

53. In Delaware, the Board of Pharmacy consists of how many public members?

    a. 3

    b. 6

    c. 7

    d. 9

54. In Delaware, what is the terms of service in the Board of pharmacy?

    a. 2 years

    b. 3 years

    c. 4 years

    d. 5 years

55. In Delaware, permanent closing of pharmacy must be notified to the Board of Pharmacy within how many days?

    a. 10 days

    b. 14 days

    c. 21 days

    d. 30 days

56. A member of the Air Force who is authorized to administer, prescribe or dispense a controlled substance during official duties is required to register with DEA on:

    a. Every 6 months

    b. Annually

    c. Biennially

    d. Exempt from registration

57. Per Federal laws, what is the maximum amount of opium a pharmacist can sell as an OTC drug?

    a. 100 ml

    b. 120 ml

    c. 240 ml

    d. 360 ml

58. How many times a refill prescription can be transferred between pharmacies sharing a real-time on-line database for Diazepam 5 mg prescription with FOUR refills on it?

    a. 3 refills

    b. 4 refills

    c. 5 refills

    d. 10 refills

59. The prescription for an inpatient of a skilled nursing facility must be rendered and at least partially filled within

_____ following the date of issue.

    a.   30 days

    b.   60 days

    c.   90 days

    d.   120 days

60. How many refills are allowed for Xanax?

    a.   3 refills in 6 months

    b.   4 refills in 6 months

    c.   5 refills in 6 months

    d.   6 refills in 5 months

61. Carisoprodol is classified as

    a.   Schedule II

    b.   Schedule III

    c.   Schedule IV

    d.   Schedule V

62. A physician's agent cannot call in for a prescription for:

    a. Lorazepam

    b. Pregabalin

    c. Dronabinol

    d. Hydromorphone

63. What is the maximum day supply of the medication the pharmacy can dispense for an emergency situation like natural disaster fill?

    a. 10 days

    b. 14 days

    c. 30 days

    d. 60 days

64. Per Federal law, what is the limit for schedule II day of supply?

    a. 30 days

    b. 90 days

    c. 120 days

    d. No limit

65. Medicaid/Medicare records of patient's are required to be stored for at least:

    a. 5 years

    b. 7 years

    c. 10 years.

    d. 12 years.

66. A prescriber may authorize a maximum of how many refills on a prescription for Percodan tablets?

    a. 0

    b. 1

    c. 2

    d. 5

    e. 10

67. What is the schedule for 200 mg of codeine in a 100 ml solution (including non-narcotic ingredients)?

    a. Schedule II

    b. Schedule III

    c. Schedule IV

    d. Schedule V

68. An exact count is allowed for schedule IV product in a container that holds greater or equal to _____ capsules or tablets.

    a. 500

    b. 1000

    c. 1500

    d. 2000

69. What is the maximum day of supply of lorazepam that may be prescribed by a physician?

    a. 30 days

    b. 60 days

    c. 90 days

    d. None of the above.

70. A prescription of Lipitor 10 mg is valid for:

    a. 3 months

    b. 6 months

    c. 9 months

    d. 12 months

71. In Delaware, what is the size of pharmacy prescription department?

   a. 120 sq. ft

   b. 180 sq. ft

   c. 250 sq. ft

   d. 300 sq. ft

72. In Delaware, temporary pharmacy permit may be granted for how many days period while the application for a permanent permit is pending?

   a. 15 days

   b. 30 days

   c. 60 days

   d. 90 days

73. In Delaware, what is the renewal time for pharmacy permit?

   a. Biennially

   b. Every three years

   c. Every four years

   d. Every 6 months

74. In Delaware, inventory records must be maintained for how long?

    a. 1 year

    b. 2 years

    c. 3 years

    d. 4 years

75. In Delaware, what is the maximum CE hours required during biennial renewal period?

    a. 20 hours

    b. 30 hours

    c. 45 hours

    d. 60 hours

76. In Delaware, when is the date of expiration of pharmacist permits?

    a. July 30

    b. September 30

    c. November 30

    d. March 30

77. In Delaware, C-II prescriptions will become void unless dispensed within how many days of the original date of the prescription?

    a. 7 days

    b. 21 days

    c. 30 days

    d. 6 months

78. In Delaware, what is the maximum supply that can be dispensed at a time for Morphine prescription?

    a. 30 dosage units

    b. 90 dosage units

    c. 100 dosage units

    d. 120 dosage units

79. In Delaware, termination of pharmacist in charge must be notified to the board of pharmacy within how many days?

    a. 5 days

    b. 10 days

    c. 15 days

    d. 30 days

80. In Delaware, change of ownership must be notified to the board of pharmacy within how many days?

    a.   10 days

    b.   15 days

    c.   30 days

    d.   45 days

81. A practitioner may dispense directly to ultimate user a controlled substance classified in Schedule II in an amount not to exceed:

    a.   48-hours supply

    b.   72-hours supply

    c.   120-hours supply

    d.   180-hours supply

82. All prescription records for non-controlled substances shall be maintained on the licensed premises for a period of _____ from the date of dispensing.

    a.   1 year

    b.   2 years

    c.   3 years

    d.   4 years

83. A prescription for Xanax is valid for:

    a.   4 months

    b.   5 months

    c.   6 months

    d.   12 months

84. A prescriber may authorize a maximum of how many refills on a prescription for Percodan tablets?

    a.   0

    b.   1

    c.   2

    d.   5

85. What is the maximum number of refills for Soma prescriptions in a six-month period?

    a.   2

    b.   3

    c.   4

    d.   5

86. Which of the following is an example of 3 file storage system?

   a. Schedule I, Schedule II- III, Schedule V

   b. Schedule II, Schedule III-V, Non-scheduled

   c. Schedule I, Schedule II- V, Non-scheduled

   d. Schedule II, Schedule III, Schedule IV, Schedule V

87. In non-emergency situations, a pharmacist may dispense an oral prescription received from a duly authorized agent of a practitioner for all of the following drugs EXCEPT:

   a. Lorazepam

   b. Lyrica

   c. Vimpat

   d. Cocaine

88. If a prescription is written for a 90-day supply, then what is the expiration term for this prescription?

   a. Original plus 2 refills

   b. Original plus 3 refills

   c. Original plus 4 refills

   d. Original plus 11 refills

89. Dr. Adam called in for emergency fill of Percocet 10/325. What do you do?

    a. Fill up to 90 days supply

    b. Don't fill

    c. Oral prescription of C-II is illegal.

    d. Physician can call in schedule II drug in case of emergency

90. When a pharmacist partially fills controlled substance II, the remaining portion of a schedule II prescription may be filled within:

    a. 24-hours of the first partial filling.

    b. 36-hours of the first partial filling.

    c. 48-hours of the first partial filling.

    d. 72-hours of the first partial filling.

91. Which of the following medications requires an exact count as an inventory?

    a. Soma

    b. Vimpat

    c. Halcion

    d. Percocet

92. According to federal law, DEA forms need to be maintained for _____ years.

    a. 1

    b. 2

    c. 5

    d. 7

93. The supplier of oxycodone 10 mg has time to send shipment to purchaser within:

    a. 10 days

    b. 15 days

    c. 30 days

    d. 60 days

94. A prescription for Xanax 2mg may be refilled how many times?

    a. 1

    b. 2

    c. 3

    d. 5

95. Which of the following is TRUE about schedule II prescription?

I. It can be refilled.

II. It can be transferred.

III. It can be faxed.

IV. It can be emailed.

  a. II only

  b. III only

  c. IV only

  d. None of the above.

96. An authorized prescriber must mail a copy of an emergency

oral prescription for a schedule II drug within_____

after an oral authorization.

  a. 72 hours

  b. 7 days

  c. 14 days

  d. 30 days

97. The prescriber is mandated to return the hardcopy prescription within _____ days after giving over the phone schedule II emergency supply per Federal law.

    a.   24 hours

    b.   72 hours

    c.   7 days

    d.   10 days

98. Recalled drugs must be removed from inventory within _____ hours of the recall notification.

    a.   12 hours

    b.   24 hours

    c.   36 hours

    d.   72 hours

99. The prescription for a terminally ill patient must be tendered and at least partially filled within_____ following the date of issue.

    a.   30 days

    b.   60 days

    c.   90 days

    d.   120 days

100.Emergency contraception treatment may be prescribed up

to_____ of unprotected intercourse.

a. 12 hours

b. 48 hours

c. 120 hours

d. 150 hours

101.The partial filling of Morphine 15 mg for terminally ill patient

must be done within _____

from the initial filling.

a. 72 hours

b. 144 hours

c. 30 days

d. 60 days

102.A pharmacist receives a prescription for 40 Percocet tablets,

but the pharmacy has only 15 tablets in stock. The patient

accepts the 15 tablets. How much time does the pharmacist

have to provide the remaining 25 tablets?

a. 24 hours

b. 72 hours

c. 96 hours

d. 6 months

103. Per Federal laws, how long does the pharmacy keep records of schedule II drugs?

    a. 2 years

    b. 3 years

    c. 5 years

    d. 7 years

104. Long-term detoxification treatment should not be longer than:

    a. 30 days

    b. 60 days

    c. 120 days

    d. 180 days

105. Per Federal laws, in order to buy pseudoephedrine related OTC Schedule V drugs, the purchaser should be at least _____ old.

    a. 16 years

    b. 18 years

    c. 21 years

    d. 23 years

106. Per Federal law what is the quantity limit of schedule II drugs to be dispensed at a time?

    a. 30 days

    b. 60 days

    c. 90 days

    d. 120 days

107. A pharmacist receives a prescription for 40 Percocet tablets, but the pharmacy has only 15 tablets in stock. The patient accepts the 15 tablets. How much time does the pharmacist have to provide the remaining 25 tablets per Federal law?

    a. 24 hours

    b. 72 hours

    c. 96 hours

    d. 6 months

108. What is the maximum day supply of the medication the pharmacy can dispense for an emergency situation like natural disaster fill?

    a. 10 days

    b. 14 days

    c. 30 days

    d. 60 days

109. Per Federal law if a prescription fails to send a cover prescription for the controlled drug, the pharmacy shall notify the Bureau of Narcotic Enforcement in writing within:

    a. 80 hours of the prescriber's failure to do so.

    b. 120 hours of the prescriber's failure to do so.

    c. 144 hours of the prescriber's failure to do so.

    d. 160 hours of the prescriber's failure to do so.

110. Medicaid/Medicare records of patient's are required to be stored for at least:

    a. 5 years

    b. 7 years

    c. 10 years.

    d. 12 years.

111. An exact count is allowed for schedule IV product in a container that holds greater or equal to _____ capsules or tablets.

    a. 500

    b. 1000

    c. 1500

    d. 2000

112.What is the maximum day of supply of lorazepam that may be

prescribed by a physician?

    a.   30 days

    b.   60 days

    c.   90 days

    d.   No limit

113.A practitioner may dispense directly to ultimate user a

controlled substance classified in Schedule II in an amount not

to exceed:

    a.   48-hours supply

    b.   72-hours supply

    c.   120-hours supply

    d.   180-hours supply

114.What is the maximum amount of codeine a pharmacist can sell

as an OTC drug within any consecutive 96-hour period?

    a.   60 ml

    b.   120 ml

    c.   180 ml

    d.   360 ml

115.When a pharmacist partially fills controlled substance II, the remaining portion of a schedule II prescription may be filled within:

   a.   24-hours of the first partial filling.

   b.   36-hours of the first partial filling.

   c.   48-hours of the first partial filling.

   d.   72-hours of the first partial filling.

116.A pharmacist receives a prescription for 40 Percocet tablets, but the pharmacy has only 15 tablets in stock. The patient accepts the 15 tablets. How much time does the pharmacist have to provide the remaining 25 tablets?

   a.   24 hours

   b.   72 hours

   c.   96 hours

   d.   6 months

117.The partial filling of a schedule II drugs for terminally ill patients must be carried out within:

   a.   10 days from the initial filling

   b.   96 hours from the initial filling.

   c.   30 days from the initial filling.

   d.   72 hours from the initial filling

118. The prescriber is mandated to return the hardcopy prescription

within _____ days after giving over the phone schedule

II emergency supply per Federal law.

    a.   24 hours

    b.   72 hours

    c.   7 days

    d.   10 days

119. Recalled drugs must be removed from inventory within

_____ hours of the recall notification.

    a.   12 hours

    b.   24 hours

    c.   36 hours

    d.   72 hours

120. The prescription for a terminally ill patient must be tendered

and at least partially filled within_____ following the

date of issue.

    a.   30 days

    b.   60 days

    c.   90 days

    d.   120 days

121. Emergency contraception treatment may be prescribed up

to_____ of unprotected intercourse.

    a.   12 hours

    b.   48 hours

    c.   120 hours

    d.   150 hours

122. OTC sales of pseudoephedrine should be maintained by a

pharmacy for:

    a.   At least one year.

    b.   At least two years.

    c.   At least three years.

    d.   At least four years.

123. In Delaware, an emergency C-II oral prescription hardcopy

must be mailed to pharmacy within how many days?

    a.   3 days

    b.   7 days

    c.   14 days

    d.   21 days

124.In Delaware, documentation of continuing education hours

(CE) must be retained for a minimum of how many years?

    a. 3 years

    b. 4 years

    c. 5 years

    d. 6 years

125.In Delaware, what is the minimum CE hours required as

"medication safety or errors"?

    a. 1 hour

    b. 2 hours

    c. 3 hours

    d. 5 hours

126.In Delaware, when can you complete a partial fill of a CII drug

beyond 72 hours?

    a. Minors

    b. Elderly

    c. Healthcare workers

    d. LTCF patients

127. In Delaware, in the event of death of owner/pharmacist-in-charge, fire or water damage when do you have to notify the Delaware executive secretary?

   a. 5 days

   b. 10 days

   c. 15 days

   d. Immediately

128. In Delaware, upon written request the license can be placed inactive status for how long?

   a. For up to 4 years

   b. For up to 5 years

   c. For up to 6 years

   d. For up to 10 years

129. In Delaware, in how many days you must get pharmacy records to a patient that has requested them?

   a. Up to 5 days

   b. Up to 10 days

   c. Up to 15 days

   d. Up to 30 days

130. In Delaware, how long do you have to keep records for an automated pharmacy system?

    a. 2 years

    b. 3 years

    c. 4 years

    d. 5 years

131. In Delaware, how long does an intern have to notify the board of change in preceptor?

    a. 5 days

    b. 10 days

    c. 15 days

    d. 30 days

132. In Delaware, how long do you have to retrieve controlled substance files upon the request of the office of controlled substance?

    a. 12 hours

    b. 36 hours

    c. 72 hours

    d. 96 hours

133. In Delaware, how long do nursing homes have to keep records for controlled substances?

    a. 2 years

    b. 3 years

    c. 5 years

    d. 6 years

134. In Delaware, how long do prescription files need to be maintained?

    a. 2 years
    b. 3 years
    c. 4 years
    d. 5 years

135. In Delaware, how long for partial filing of C-II required?

    a. 24 hours fill must be completed and if remaining portion cannot be filled prescriber must notify the physician.

    b. 48 hours fill must be completed and if remaining portion cannot be filled prescriber must notify the physician.

    c. 72 hours fill must be completed and if remaining portion cannot be filled prescriber must notify the physician.

    d. 120 hours fill must be completed and if remaining portion cannot be filled prescriber must notify the physician.

136.In Delaware. what requirements need to be put on a partial filled C-II for LTCF or terminally Ill patient?

I. Date of partial fill.

II. Quantity dispensed.

III. Remaining quantity authorized.

IV. Identification of dispensing pharmacist.

    a. I only

    b. II and III only

    c. II, III and IV only

    d. I, II, III and IV only

137.In Delaware, how many years must a pharmacist have to practice to become a preceptor?

    a. Minimum of 3 years

    b. Minimum of 6 years

    c. Minimum of 1 year

    d. Minimum of 2 years

138.In Delaware, how many days required to notify board change of preceptor?

    a. Within 5 days

    b. Within 10 days

    c. Within 15 days

    d. Within 30 days

139. In Delaware, when must the pharmacy provider be contacted after emergency use medications are used in a nursing home?

   a. 6 hours

   b. 12 hours

   c. 24 hours

   d. 48 hours

140. In Delaware, how long must the provider pharmacy maintain emergency use medication records in a nursing home?

   a. Minimum of 1 year

   b. Minimum of 2 years

   c. Minimum of 3 years

   d. Minimum of 4 years

141. In Delaware, how many people are needed to destroy unused controlled patient medications in a nursing home?

   a. 2 authorized licensed personnel

   b. 3 authorized licensed personnel

   c. 4 authorized licensed personnel

   d. 5 authorized licensed personnel

142. In Delaware, how many time can the board grant a 90-day extension of a temporary pharmacist license?

   a. Once

   b. Twice

   c. Three times

   d. Not allowed at all

143. In Delaware, what are the main requirements to register an applicant as a pharmacy, distributor, manufacturer, practitioner, researcher, or other controlled substance registrant for purposes of manufacturing, distributing or dispensing, some or all of the controlled substances included in Schedules I-V?

   I. Maintenance of effective controls against diversion of controlled substances into other than legitimate medical, scientific or industrial channels.

   II. Compliance with applicable federal, state and local law, including but not limited to such requirements as having a license to practice as a practitioner or having documented training and continuing education as a drug detection animal trainer.

III. Any convictions of the applicant under any federal and state laws relating to any controlled substance.

IV. Any professional license disciplined in any jurisdiction.

    a. I and II only

    b. II and III only

    c. III and IV only

    d. I, II, III, and V only

144. In Delaware, what is the maximum time given before denying, suspending or revoking a registration, the Secretary shall serve upon the applicant or registrant an order to show cause why registration should not be denied, suspended or revoked?

    a. 15 days

    b. 30 days

    c. 45 days

    d. 60 days

145. In Delaware, what are the grounds for limitation, suspension, or revocation of registration? Those who:

I. Has failed to comply with applicable federal, state, or local law.

II. Has been convicted under any federal or state law relating to any controlled substances.

III. Has been disciplined by a professional licensing board in any jurisdiction.

IV. Has engaged in any conduct the Secretary finds to be relevant and inconsistent with the public interest.

    a. I and II only

    b. II and III only

    c. III and IV only

    d. I, II, III, and IV only

146. In Delaware, a controlled substance included in Schedule III or IV which is a prescription drug shall not be valid for more than how many months?

    a. 3 months

    b. 6 months

    c. 12 months

    d. 18 months

147. In Delaware, what is the maximum quantity that can be sold within 30 days?

a. 3.5 grams

b. 7.5 grams

c. 9 grams

d. 12 grams

148. In Delaware, the pharmacy or retailer shall maintain a written or electronic log of required information for each sale of a nonprescription product containing pseudoephedrine or ephedrine, product?

I. The date and time of any transaction.

II. The name, address, and date of birth of the person purchasing or obtaining the substance.

III. The type of government-issued identification provided by the person purchasing or obtaining the substance and identification number.

IV. The government agency issuing the identification used; and

a. I and II only

b. II and III only

c. III and IV only

d. I, II, III, and IV only

149. In Delaware, what is the age limit for sale of

dextromethorphan?

    a.   16 years or over

    b.   17 years or over

    c.   18 years or over

    d.   21 years or over

150. In Delaware, what is the CE hours required during each full

licensure renewal period between October 1 to September 30

even-numbered years?

    a.   10 days

    b.   15 days

    c.   30 days

    d.   45 days

151. In Delaware, what is the CE hours required in "medication

safety/errors"?

    a.   1 hour

    b.   2 hours

    c.   3 hours

    d.   5 hours

152.In Delaware, what is the CE hours required in administering

"injectable medications, biological and adult immunizations"?

    a. 1 hour

    b. 2 hours

    c. 3 hours

    d. 5 hours

153.In Delaware, what is the CE hours required in the

"distribution, dispensing or delivery of controlled substances"?

    a. 1 hour

    b. 2 hours

    c. 3 hours

    d. 5 hours

ANSWER TO PART ONE

1. Answer is (A)

    - Who appoints the board members in Delaware?

    - The governor

2. Answer is (C)

    - Who can counsel a patient or a patient's agent?

    - A pharmacist

    - A pharmacy interns

3. Answer is C

    - A pharmacy must retain prescriptions for at least:

    - Three years.

4. Answer is (E)

    - A pharmacist must administer an authorized vaccine using:

    - A standing order.

    - A protocol.

    - A prescription.

5. Answer is E

- A pharmacist shall attain a minimum of 500 hours under supervision of a nuclear pharmacist furthermore the pharmacist shall receive a minimum of 200 hours of instruction from an accredited college of pharmacy

6. The correct answer is D

- Only pharmacist practicing at the pharmacy and the pharmacist-in-charge shall have access to keys or other means of opening the pharmacy or alarm access code

7. Answer is E

- In Delaware pharmacy technicians are Not required to be

- Licensed.

- Registered

- Certified

8. Answer is B

- A pharmacist who wants to register as a nuclear pharmacist must have received a minimum of 200 contact hours of didactic instruction in nuclear pharmacy

9. The correct answer is C

- Pharmacies located outside of Delaware may not ship, mail, or deliver prescription drugs into Delaware without first obtaining a Delaware pharmacy per licensure, a non-resident pharmacy must be located in the United States or a U.S. territory.

10. Answer: D

- Does Delaware require a prescription to buy insulin syringes?
- Some regions may require a prescription.
- Not required, if the purchaser is at least 18 years old.

11. Answer is B

- Pen needles for the administration of prescription medications by injection in the State of Delaware doesn't need a prescription, but only sold to persons who have attained the age of 18 years.

12. Answer: C

- 9 grams of pseudoephedrine in a 30-day period.

13. Answer is C

- For each partial filling, the dispensing pharmacist shall record on the back of the prescription (or another appropriate record uniformly maintained, and readily retrievable) the date of the partial filling, quantity dispensed, remaining quantity authorized to be dispensed and the identification of the dispensing pharmacist

14. The correct answer is B

   - What is the data collection interval under the

     prescription drug monitoring program?

   - Within 24 hours of dispensing.

15. Answer is C

   - Only Interns and pharmacist can perform drug

     utilization review.

16. Answer is D

   - If a pharmacy is going to be closed for more than seven

     consecutive business days, the Board must be notified

     5 days prior to the temporary closing.

17. Answer is D

   - For a pharmacist, at least how many hours of

     continuing education per biennial licensure period must

     be in the area of medication safely/errors?

   - At least 2 hours

18. Answer is (C)

- Delaware requires oral counselling in certain situations or an "offer to counsel" It requires documentation of "offer to counsel" lt requires documentation of patient's refusal for counseling. It DOES NOT require to counsel refills. It requires an appropriate process for counselling when a patient le not in the pharmacy. It requires to discuss with a patient prior generic substitution. It requires distribution of written materials.

19. Answer is B

- Records related to an Automated Pharmacy System shall be kept for a period of

- Three years.

20. Answer is (A)

- Hon many 1times a refill prescription can be transferred between pharmacies sharing. a real-time on-line database fora schedule Il drug. prescriptions with five refills on?

- A maximum of five refills

21. Answer: B

- Under the Combat Methamphetamine Epidemic Act of 2005, the maximum amount of pseudoephedrine that may purchase in a single day is 3.6 g; the maximum amount that may be purchased in a 30-day time period is 9 g.

22. Answer: A

- Schedule I includes drugs such as Marijuana, Ecstasy, Peyote, and Heroin.

23. Answer: D

- According to the Controlled Substances Act, a physician has up to 7 calendar days to provide a pharmacy a handwritten prescription for a Sched- ule II medication if it was called in to the pharmacy. The quantity prescribed should be enough to last only until the patient can see the physician.

24. Answer: D

- The telephone number is not required on the prescription label, but it is required on the prescription.

25. Answer: B

- A prescription may only be transferred one time from one pharmacy to another pharmacy of the number of refills remaining. When the prescription is transferred, the original pharmacy notes on the prescription that it has been transferred and is now void.

26. Answer: B

- Tylenol with codeine (acetaminophen with codeine) is classified as a Schedule III medication by the Drug Enforcement Administration.

27. Answer: A

- CIII drugs can have up to 5 refills and are refillable up to 6 months. Some examples of C-IV drugs include Xanax.

28. Answer: A

- Schedule I drug has no medical use.

29. Answer: B

- 1.8 grams of codeine in a 100 ml solution is a schedule III drug.

30. Answer: A

- Per Federal laws, the pharmacy keeps records of schedule II drugs for 2 years

31. Answer: D

- Long-term detoxification treatment should not be longer than 6 months or 180 days.

32. Answer: B

- Per Federal laws, the purchaser should be at least 18 years old.

33. Answer: C

- A pharmacy may dispense accelerated refills of up to a 90-day supply of medication pursuant to a valid prescription that may be dispensed with authorized refills, as long as it doesn't exceed the total quantity authorized by the prescriber.

34. Answer: C

- There is 90-day supply limit to all schedule II drugs per federal laws.

35. Answer: B

- 500 mg of opium in a 100 ml solution is a schedule III drug.

36. Answer is B

- Records of pseudoephedrine sales shall be maintained by the pharmacy for

- At least one year.

37. Answer is D

- If a computerized system is used to maintain.

  Prescription records it shall be designed so that the

  pharmacy can receive the printout within 5 days after

  requesting the printout.

38. Answer is A

- Schedule II Controlled Substances can be stored in a

  secured in a securely locked cabinet.

39. Answer is C

  - Immunization prescriptions must be maintained for at least

  - 3 years

40. Answer is (E)

  - A pharmacist can administer any vaccine in Delaware

41. Answer: B

  - Prescription for controlled substances in schedules II and will become void unless dispensed within seven (7) days of the original date of the prescription or unless the original prescriber authorizes the prescription past the seven (7) day period

42. Answer is D

  - In Delaware pharmacist licenses expire on September 30 of even years

43. Answer is E

- Who can dispense a product containing pseudoephedrine without a prescription?

- A pharmacy clerks

- A pharmacy technician

- A pharmacy in term

44. Answer C

- How many hours of CEs are required to collect by a pharmacist per renewal period?

- 30 hours

45. Answer A

- Such prescription may be dispensed up to 100 dosage units.

46. Answer: B

- Such prescription may be dispensed up to 100 dosage units or a 31-day supply whatever is the greater.

47. Answer B.

- A pharmacy permit holder shall write the Executive of the Delaware state board of pharmacy at least 14 days in advance to anticipate the ceasing operation as licensed pharmacy.

48. Answer D.

- The practical filling of schedule II-controlled substances should be done within 72 hours from the initial filling However for LTCF patients or for the terminally ill patient schedule II substances can be partially filled up to 60 days the from the original date of the prescription

49. Answer A

- Following health professionals CANNOT possess controlled substances in Delaware

- Doctor of homeopathy

- Midwives

- Optometrists

- Naturopathic doctors

- Pharmacists

50. Answer D

- How many hours of practical experience are required

  by an intern?

- At least 1500 hours of Internship

51. Answer B

- Such prescription must be mailed within 7 days of

  such authorization

52. Answer: D

- Board of pharmacy consists of 9 members.

53. Answer: A

- In Delaware, the Board of Pharmacy consists of 3

  public members.

54. Answer: B

- In Delaware, the terms of service in the Board of pharmacy are 3 years.

55. Answer: B

- Closing pharmacy

- If permanent, must notify the BOP 14 days prior to closing

- If temporary, if more than 7 days then BOP must be notified 5 days prior to temporary closing

56. Answer: D

- The requirement of registration is waived for any official or agency of the U.S. Army, Navy, Marine Corps, Air Force, Coast Guard, or Public Health Service who or which is authorized to import or export-controlled substances in the course of his or her official duties.

57. Answer: C

- 240 ml of opium can be sold by pharmacist as an OTC drug.

58. Answer: B

- A maximum of 4 refill prescription can be transferred between pharmacies sharing a real-time on-line database for a schedule IV drug prescription like diazepam 5 mg with FOUR refills on it.

59. Answer: B

- The prescription for an inpatient of a skilled nursing facility must be rendered and at least partially filled within 60 days following the date of issue.

60. Answer: C

- Xanax is classified as controlled substances (schedule IV).

61. Answer: C

- Carisoprodol- Schedule IV.

62. Answer: D

- A physician's agent cannot call for schedule II drugs. In this case, hydromorphone.

63. Answer: C

- The maximum day supply of the medication the pharmacy can dispense for an emergency situation like natural disaster fill is 30 days' supply.

64. Answer: D

- Per Federal law, there is no limit for schedule II day of supply.

65. Answer is C

- Records related to Medicaid/Medicare patients are required to be stored for at least. 10 years.

66. Answer: A

- Schedule II drugs has no refills.

67. Answer: D

- 200 mg/100 ml of codeine solution is a schedule V drug.

68. Answer: B

- An exact count is allowed for schedule III- V products in a container that holds greater or equal to 1000 capsules or tablets.

69. Answer: D

- There is no limit on the quantity of schedule III-V controlled substances that can be prescribed by a physician.

70. Answer: D

- A prescription of Lipitor 10 mg is valid for 12 months or 1 year.

71. Answer: C

- Pharmacy space requirements: a prescription department must have at least 250 square feet of floor space.

72. Answer: C

- Temporary pharmacy permit may be granted for a 60-day period while the application for a permanent permit is pending. An additional 60-day period may be granted as extension.

73. Answer: A

- Renewal of pharmacy permit must be renewed biennially.

74. Answer: B

- In Delaware, inventory records must be maintained for 2 years.

75. Answer: B

- In Delaware, the number of continuing education units (CEUs) required for re-licensure shall not exceed 3 CEUs during any biennial registration

76. Answer: B

- In Delaware, date of expiration of pharmacy permits is on

- September 30

77. Answer: A

- In Delaware, C-II and CIII prescriptions will become void unless dispensed within 7 days of the original date of the prescription.

78. Answer: C

- Cannot be written nor dispensed for more than 100 dosage units or a 31-day supply, whichever is greater.

79. Answer: B

- Notify Board of pharmacy within 10 days of termination of pharmacist in charge.

80. Answer: A

- Notify Board of pharmacy within 10 days of change of ownership.

81. Answer: B

- A practitioner may dispense directly to un ultimate user a controlled substance classified in Schedule II in an amount not to exceed 72-hours supply.

82. Answer: A

- All prescription records for non-controlled substances shall be maintained on the licensed premises for a period of one year from the date of dispensing.

83. Answer: C

- A prescription for schedule III to IV is valid for 6 months.

84. Answer: A

- Schedule II drugs has no refills.

85. Answer: D

- Soma has 5 refills, schedule IV.

86. Answer: B

- 3 file storage system means: Schedule II, Schedule III-V, Non-scheduled.

87. Answer: D

- Schedule II drugs don't be dispensed via oral prescription in non-emergency situations.

88. Answer: B

- 90 days = 1 months plus 3 refills

89. Answer: D

- Over the phone prescription of schedule II drugs can be filled in case of emergency.

90. Answer: D

- When a pharmacist partially fills controlled substance II, the remaining portion of a schedule II prescription may be filled within 72-hours of the first partial filling.

91. Answer: D

- Schedule II drug Percocet requires an exact count for inventory.

92. Answer: B

- According to federal law, DEA forms need to be maintained for 2 years.

93. Answer: D

- The supplier of oxycodone 10 mg has time to send shipment to purchaser within 60 days.

94. Answer: D

- Schedule 4 drug and can be refilled 5 times.

95. Answer: D

- It cannot be refilled, transferred or faxed it can be faxed only on few exceptions.

96. Answer is B

- Such prescription must be mailed within 7 days of such authorization.

97. Answer: C

- The prescriber is mandated to return the hardcopy prescription within SEVEN days after giving over the phone schedule II emergency supply.

98. Answer: B

- Recalled drugs must be removed from inventory within 24 hours of the recall notification.

99. Answer: B

- The prescription for a terminally ill patient must be tendered and at least partially filled within 60 days following the date of issue.

100. Answer: C

- Emergency contraception treatment may be prescribed up to 120 hours of unprotected intercourse.

101. Answer: D

- The partial filling of Morphine 15 mg for terminally ill patient must be done within 60 days from the initial filling.

102. Answer: B

- The Controlled Substances Act allows for the partial filling of a Schedule II medication prescription, with the remaining medication to be provided to the patient within 72 hours or the quantity becomes void.

103. Answer: A

- Per Federal laws, the pharmacy keeps records of schedule II drugs for 2 years

104. Answer: D

- Long-term detoxification treatment should not be longer than 6 months or 180 days.

105. Answer: B

- Per Federal laws, the purchaser should be at least 18 years old.

106. Answer: C

- There is 90-day supply limit to all schedule II drugs per federal laws.

107. Answer: B

- The Controlled Substances Act allows for the partial filling of a Schedule II medication prescription, with the remaining medication to be provided to the patient within 72 hours or the quantity becomes void.

108.Answer: C

- The maximum day supply of the medication the pharmacy can dispense for an emergency situation like natural disaster fill is 30 days' supply.

109.Answer: C

- If a prescription fails to send a cover prescription for the controlled drug, the pharmacy shall notify the Bureau of Narcotic Enforcement in writing within 144 hours of the prescriber's failure to do so.

110.Answer is C

- Records related to Medicaid/Medicare patients are required to be stored for at least 10 years.

111.Answer: B

- An exact count is allowed for schedule III- V products in a container that holds greater or equal to 1000 capsules or tablets.

112.Answer: D

- There is no limit on the quantity of schedule III-V controlled substances that can be prescribed by a physician.

113.Answer: B

- A practitioner may dispense directly to un ultimate user a controlled substance classified in Schedule II in an amount not to exceed 72-hours supply.

114.Answer: B

- No person shall obtain or attempt to obtain within any consecutive 96 hours period any Schedule V substances of more than 120 milliliters or more than 120 grams containing codeine.

115.Answer: D

- When a pharmacist partially fills controlled substance II, the remaining portion of a schedule II prescription may be filled within 72-hours of the first partial filling.

116.Answer: B

- The Controlled Substances Act allows for the partial filling of a Schedule II medication pre- scription, with the remaining medication to be provided to the patient within 72 hours or the quantity becomes void.

117.Answer is D.

- The practical filling of schedule II-controlled substances should be done within 72 hours from the initial filling However for LTCF patients or for the terminally ill patient schedule II substances can be partially filled up to 60 days the from the original date of the prescription

118. Answer: C

- The prescriber is mandated to return the hardcopy

  prescription within SEVEN days after giving over the

  phone schedule II emergency supply.

119. Answer: B

- Recalled drugs must be removed from inventory within 24

  hours of the recall notification.

120. Answer: B

- The prescription for a terminally ill patient must be

  tendered and at least partially filled within 60 days

  following the date of issue.

121. Answer: C

- Emergency contraception treatment may be prescribed up

  to 120 hours of unprotected intercourse.

122. Answer: B

- OTC sales of pseudoephedrine should be maintained by a

  pharmacy for at least 2 years.

123. Answer: B

- In Delaware, an emergency C-II oral prescription hardcopy must be mailed to pharmacy within 7 days of oral authorization.

124. Answer: D

- In Delaware, documentation of continuing education hours (CE) must be retained for a minimum of 6 years.

125. Answer: B

- In Delaware, continuing education required is at least 2 hours on medication safety/errors.

126. Answer: D

- For pts who are terminally ill or reside in a LTCF- can complete the partial fill up to 60 days from the date the prescription was written.

127.Answer: D

- In the event of death of owner/pharmacist-in-charge, fire or water damage, you have to notify the Delaware executive secretary immediately.

128.Answer: A

- In Delaware, upon written request the license can be placed inactive status for 4 years.

129.Answer: C

- In Delaware, in 15 days you must get pharmacy records to a patient that has requested them.

130.Answer: B

- In Delaware, you have to keep records for an automated pharmacy system for 3 years.

131.Answer: B

- In Delaware, an intern has to notify the board of change in preceptor within 10 days.

132.Answer: C

- In DE, you have to retrieve controlled substance files upon the request of the office of controlled substance within 72 hours.

133.Answer: A

- In Delaware, nursing homes have to keep records for controlled substances for 2 years.

134.Answer: B

- In Delaware, prescription files need to be maintained for 3 years.

135.Answer: C

- In Delaware, partial filing of C-II require 72 hours fill must be completed and if remaining portion cannot be filled prescriber must notify the physician.

89

136.Answer: D

- In Delaware. what requirements need to be put on a

  partial filled C-II for LTCF or terminally Ill patient?

- Date of partial fill.

- Quantity dispensed.

- Remaining quantity authorized.

- Identification of dispensing pharmacist.

137.Answer: D

- In Delaware, a pharmacist has to practice a minimum
  of 2 years to become a preceptor.

138.Answer: B

- In Delaware, change of preceptor must be notified to
  the board within 10 days.

139.Answer: C

- In Delaware, the pharmacy provider be contacted 24
  hours after emergency use medications are used in a
  nursing home.

140. Answer: B

- In Delaware, the provider pharmacy maintains for minimum of 2 years in emergency use medication records in a nursing home.

141. Answer: A

- In Delaware, 2 authorized licensed personnel are needed to destroy unused controlled patient medications in a nursing home.

142. Answer: A

- In Delaware, the board grant a 90-day extension of a temporary pharmacist license only once.

143. Answer: D

- § 4733. Registration; rights of registrants.

- The Secretary shall register an applicant as a pharmacy, distributor, manufacturer, practitioner, researcher or other controlled substance registrant for purposes of manufacturing, distributing or dispensing, some or all of

the controlled substances included in Schedules I-V who

has an active, relevant underlying professional license in

the State unless the Secretary determines that the issuance

of that registration would be inconsistent with the public

interest. In determining the public interest, the Secretary

shall consider the following factors:

a. Maintenance of effective controls against diversion of

controlled substances into other than legitimate

medical, scientific or industrial channels.

b. Compliance with applicable federal, state and local

law, including but not limited to such requirements as

having a license to practice as a practitioner or having

documented training and continuing education as a

drug detection animal trainer.

c. Any convictions of the applicant under any federal and state laws relating to any controlled substance.

d. Past experience in the manufacture or distribution of controlled substances and the existence in the applicant's establishment of effective controls against diversion.

e. Furnishing by the applicant of false or fraudulent material in any application filed under this chapter.

f. Suspension or revocation of the applicant's federal registration to manufacture, distribute, prescribe, dispense or research-controlled substances as authorized by federal law.

g. Any professional license disciplined in any jurisdiction; and

h. Any other factors relevant to the public interest.

- (b) Registration under subsection (a) does not entitle a registrant to manufacture, research and distribute controlled substances in Schedule I or II other than those specified in the registration.

- (c) Practitioners must be registered to dispense any controlled substances or to conduct research with controlled substances in Schedules II through V if they are authorized to dispense or conduct research under the law of this State. The Secretary need not require separate registration under this subchapter for practitioners engaging in research with nonnarcotic controlled substances in Schedules II through V where the registrant is already registered under this subchapter in another capacity. Practitioners registered under federal law to conduct research with Schedule I substances may conduct research with Schedule I substances within this State upon furnishing the Secretary evidence of that federal

registration.

- (d) Compliance by manufacturers and distributors with the

  federal law respecting registration (excluding fees) entitles

  them to be registered under this chapter.

- 16 Del. C. 1953, § 4733; 58 Del. Laws, c. 424, § 1; 70

  Del. Laws, c. 186, § 1; 71 Del. Laws, c. 288, § 8; 79

  Del. Laws, c. 164, § 1;

144. Answer: B

- (b) Before denying, suspending or revoking a registration,

  the Secretary shall serve upon the applicant or registrant an

  order to show cause why registration should not be denied,

  suspended or revoked. The order to show cause shall

  contain a statement of the basis therefore and shall call

  upon the applicant or registrant to appear before the

  Secretary at a time and place not more than 30 days after

the date of service of the order. Proceedings to refuse

renewal of registration shall not abate the existing

registration which shall remain in effect pending the

outcome of the administrative hearing.

- 16 Del. C. 1953, §§ 4734, 4735; 58 Del. Laws, c. 424, §

  1; 60 Del. Laws, c. 583, § 4; 70 Del. Laws, c. 186, §

  1; 71 Del. Laws, c. 88, § 9; 79 Del. Laws, c. 164, § 1;

145. Answer: D

- § 4735. Investigations; written complaints; grounds for

  limitation, suspension or revocation of registration.

- All complaints shall be received and investigated by the

  Division of Professional Regulation in accordance with §

  8735 of Title 29, and the Division of Professional

  Regulation shall be responsible for issuing a final written

  report at the conclusion of its investigation.

- The Secretary, after due notice and hearing may limit, suspend, fine or revoke the registration of any registrant who:

  a. Has failed to maintain effective controls against diversion of controlled substances into other than legitimate medical, scientific, or industrial channels.

  b. Has failed to comply with applicable federal, state or local law.

  c. Has been convicted under any federal or state law relating to any controlled substances.

  d. Has furnished any false or fraudulent material in any application filed under this chapter.

  e. Has had any federal registration to manufacture, distribute, prescribe, dispense or research-controlled substances as authorized by federal law

suspended or revoked.

f. Has violated a provision of this chapter or

violated an order or rule of the Secretary related to

controlled substances.

g. Has been disciplined by a professional licensing

board in any jurisdiction; or

h. Has engaged in any conduct the Secretary finds to

be relevant and inconsistent with the public

interest.

- The Secretary may limit revocation or suspension of a

registration to particular controlled substances.

- The Secretary may fine any registrant in an amount not

to exceed $1,000 per violation of this chapter or the

rules promulgated hereunder.

- If the Secretary suspends or revokes a registration, all controlled substances owned or possessed by the registrant at the time of suspension, or the effective date of the revocation order may be placed under seal. No disposition may be made of substances under seal until the time for taking an appeal has elapsed or until all appeals have been concluded unless a court upon application therefore orders the sale of perishable substances and the deposit of the proceeds of the sale with the court. Upon a revocation order becoming final, all controlled substances may be forfeited to the State.

- (f) The Secretary shall promptly notify the Administration of all orders suspending or revoking registration and all forfeitures of controlled substances.

- 16 Del. C. 1953, § 4735; 58 Del. Laws, c. 424, § 1; 60 Del. Laws, c. 583, § 5; 70 Del. Laws, c. 186, § 1; 79 Del. Laws, c. 164, § 1;

146.Answer: B

- § 4739. Prescriptions [For application of the section, see 79 Del. Laws, c. 409, § 3].

- Except when dispensed directly by a practitioner other than a pharmacy to an ultimate user, no controlled substance in Schedule II may be dispensed without the written prescription of a practitioner.

- In emergency situations, as defined by rule of the Secretary, Schedule II drugs may be dispensed upon oral prescription of a practitioner, reduced promptly to writing and filed by the pharmacy. Prescriptions shall be retained in conformity with the requirements of this chapter. No prescription for a Schedule II substance may be refilled.

- Except when dispensed directly by a practitioner other than a pharmacy to an ultimate user, a controlled substance included in Schedule III or IV which is a prescription drug shall not be dispensed without a written or oral prescription of a practitioner. The prescription shall not be filled or refilled more than 6 months after the date thereof or be refilled more than 5 times, unless renewed by the practitioner.

- A controlled substance included in Schedule V shall not be distributed or dispensed other than for a medical purpose.

- An ultimate user shall be permitted to prohibit or limit a person other than the ultimate user from receiving a prescription on the ultimate user's behalf from a pharmacy.

- 16 Del. C. 1953, § 4738; 58 Del. Laws, c. 424, § 1; 60 Del. Laws, c. 583, § 5; 79 Del. Laws, c. 164, § 1; 79 Del. Laws, c. 409, § 1;

- § 4739A. Practitioners.

- Except for pharmacies, opioid treatment programs (also known as methadone clinics), veterinarians and persons licensed, registered, or otherwise authorized to conduct research, no practitioner shall dispense controlled substances beyond the amount deemed medically necessary for a 72-hour supply.

- 79 Del. Laws, c. 92, § 2; 80 Del. Laws, c. 5, § 1;

147.Answer: C

- § 4740. Sale of pseudoephedrine or ephedrine.

- Beginning January 1, 2014, before completing a sale of an over-the-counter material, compound, mixture, or preparation containing any detectable quantity of pseudoephedrine or ephedrine, its salts or optical isomers, or salts of optical isomers a pharmacy or retailer shall electronically submit the information required pursuant to subsection (b) of this section to the National Precursor Log Exchange system (NPLEx) administered by the National Association of Drug Diversion Investigators; provided that the NPLEx is available to pharmacies or retailers in the State without a charge for accessing the system. The pharmacy or retailer shall not complete the sale if the NPLEx system generates a stop sale alert. The system shall contain an override function that may be used by an agent of a retail establishment who is dispensing the drug product and who has a reasonable fear of imminent bodily harm if the transaction is not completed. The system shall create a record of each use of the override mechanism.

- The pharmacy or retailer shall maintain a written or electronic log of required information for each sale of a nonprescription product containing pseudoephedrine or

ephedrine, including:

- o   The date and time of any transaction.

- o   The name, address, and date of birth of the

    person purchasing or obtaining the substance.

- o   The type of government-issued identification

    provided by the person purchasing or obtaining

    the substance and identification number.

- o   The government agency issuing the identification

    used; and

- o   The name of the compound, mixture, or

    preparation and the amount.

- The pharmacy or retailer shall require every person

  purchasing or obtaining the substance to sign a written or

  electronic log attesting to the validity of the information.

- If a pharmacy or retailer selling an over-the-counter product containing the substance experiences mechanical or electronic failure of the electronic tracking system and is unable to comply with the electronic sales tracking requirement under this section, the pharmacy or retailer shall maintain a written log or an alternative electronic record keeping mechanism until such time as the pharmacy or retailer is able to comply with the electronic sales tracking requirement.

- Any material, compound, mixture, or preparation as defined in subsection (a) of this section shall be dispensed, offered for sale, sold, or distributed only from behind a checkout counter, pharmacy counter, or in a locked storage container where the public is not permitted.

- A licensed pharmacist, salesclerk, or pharmacy technician shall require that any person purchasing, receiving, or otherwise acquiring any such substance shall be age 18 or older, produce a photo identification showing the date of birth of the person, and sign a written log or receipt showing the date of the transaction, name of the person, and the amount of such substance. The written log or electronic log shall be retained for at least 12 months.

- No person, other than pharmacy or retail establishment, shall purchase, receive, or otherwise acquire more than 9 grams of any such substance within any 30-day period.

- A violation of this section is a class A misdemeanor.

- The National Association of Drug Diversion Investigators shall forward Delaware transaction records in the NPLEx to the Drug Diversion Unit of the Delaware State Police weekly and provide real-time access to the NPLEx information through the NPLEx online

portal to law enforcement in the State as authorized by

the State Police; provided that the State Police execute a

memorandum of understanding with the National

Association of Drug Diversion Investigators governing

access to the information; provided further that the State

Police shall establish the electronic tracking system in

conjunction with the State's existing narcotics tracking

system no later than January 1, 2014.

- 75 Del. Laws, c. 52, § 1; 75 Del. Laws, c. 217, § 1; 77

  Del. Laws, c. 334, § 1; 79 Del. Laws, c. 175, § 1;

148. Answer: D

- § 4740. Sale of pseudoephedrine or ephedrine.

- Beginning January 1, 2014, before completing a sale of an

  over-the-counter material, compound, mixture, or

  preparation containing any detectable quantity of

pseudoephedrine or ephedrine, its salts or optical isomers,

or salts of optical isomers a pharmacy or retailer shall

electronically submit the information required pursuant to

subsection (b) of this section to the National Precursor

Log Exchange system (NPLEx) administered by the

National Association of Drug Diversion Investigators;

provided that the NPLEx is available to pharmacies or

retailers in the State without a charge for accessing the

system. The pharmacy or retailer shall not complete the

sale if the NPLEx system generates a stop sale alert. The

system shall contain an override function that may be used

by an agent of a retail establishment who is dispensing the

drug product and who has a reasonable fear of imminent

bodily harm if the transaction is not completed. The

system shall create a record of each use of the override

mechanism.

- The pharmacy or retailer shall maintain a written or electronic log of required information for each sale of a nonprescription product containing pseudoephedrine or ephedrine, including:

  o The date and time of any transaction.

  o The name, address, and date of birth of the person purchasing or obtaining the substance.

  o The type of government-issued identification provided by the person purchasing or obtaining the substance and identification number.

  o The government agency issuing the identification used; and

  o The name of the compound, mixture, or preparation and the amount.

- The pharmacy or retailer shall require every person purchasing or obtaining the substance to sign a written or electronic log attesting to the validity of the information.

- If a pharmacy or retailer selling an over-the-counter product containing the substance experiences mechanical or electronic failure of the electronic tracking system and is unable to comply with the electronic sales tracking requirement under this section, the pharmacy or retailer shall maintain a written log or an alternative electronic record keeping mechanism until such time as the pharmacy or retailer is able to comply with the electronic sales tracking requirement.

- Any material, compound, mixture, or preparation as defined in subsection (a) of this section shall be dispensed, offered for sale, sold, or distributed only from behind a checkout counter, pharmacy counter, or in a locked storage container where the public is not permitted.

- A licensed pharmacist, salesclerk, or pharmacy technician shall require that any person purchasing, receiving, or otherwise acquiring any such substance shall be age 18 or older, produce a photo identification showing the date of birth of the person, and sign a written log or receipt showing the date of the transaction, name of the person, and the amount of such substance. The written log or electronic log shall be retained for at least 12 months.

- No person, other than pharmacy or retail establishment, shall purchase, receive, or otherwise acquire more than 9 grams of any such substance within any 30-day period.

- A violation of this section is a class A misdemeanor.

149. Answer: C

- § 4740A. Sale of dextromethorphan.

- *Age limit on sale of dextromethorphan.* — (1) No commercial entity shall knowingly or willfully sell or trade a finished drug product containing any quantity of dextromethorphan to a person less than 18 years of age.

- (2) No person who is less than 18 years of age shall purchase a finished drug product containing any quantity of dextromethorphan.

(3) Any person making a retail sale of a finished drug product containing any quantity of dextromethorphan shall require and obtain proof of age from the purchaser before completing the sale, unless from the purchaser's outward appearance the person making the sale would reasonably presume the purchaser to be at least 25 years of age.

- (b) *Limitations.* — (1) Nothing in this section shall be construed to impose any compliance requirement on a retail entity other than manually obtaining and verifying proof of age as a condition of sale, including placement of products in a specific place within a store, restrictions on a consumer's direct access to finished drug products, and maintenance of transaction records.

(2) This section shall not apply to a medication containing dextromethorphan that is sold pursuant to a valid prescription.

(c) *Penalties.* — Any manufacturer, distributor, retailer, or wholesaler that sells or trades dextromethorphan in violation of this section shall receive a warning letter from the Office of Controlled Substances for the first violation and thereafter be subject to a civil penalty issued by the Office of Controlled Substances in the amount of:

(1) Not more than $150 for a second violation; or

(2) Not more than $250 for a third or any subsequent

violations.

- 80 Del. Laws, c. 264, § 2;

- § 4740B. Use, distribution and education concerning

  benzodiazepine and non-benzodiazepine hypnotics.

  - *Obligations of the Secretary.* — The Secretary shall produce

    and distribute either in written or electronic form to

    pharmacies, not including institutional pharmacies,

    pamphlets for consumers relative to benzodiazepines

    and non-benzodiazepine hypnotics that includes

    educational information about:

    o   Misuse and abuse by adults and children.

    o   Risk of dependency and addiction.

    o   Proper storage and disposal.

    o   Addiction support and treatment resources; and

- o   A telephone helpline.

- A pharmacist shall distribute the pamphlet when dispensing a benzodiazepines or a non-benzodiazepine hypnotic.

  - *Duties of practitioners.* — No practitioner shall prescribe a benzodiazepine or a non-benzodiazepine hypnotic to a minor without first obtaining a parent or guardian's written informed consent except in the case of emergency treatment or for treatment associated with neuromuscular disabilities. The Secretary shall prescribe a form for physicians to use in obtaining such consent. The form shall be written in a manner designed to permit a person unfamiliar with medical terminology to understand its purpose and content, and shall include the following information:

    - Misuse and abuse by adults and children.

- Risk of dependency and addiction.

- Possible life-threatening risks of minors using the drug for the first time; and

- Risks associated with long-term use of drugs.

150.Answer: C

- Continuing Education Requirement

- The amount of continuing education (CE) that you are required to complete depends on when your license was issued during the full licensure period. If it is your first renewal, you are required to complete:

- 1.25 hours for each month between the initial date of licensure and the biennial renewal date

- Active Pharmacist licensees must complete 30 hours of approved CE during each full licensure renewal period between October 1 to September 30

116

even-numbered years (2020-2022, etc.) and must

include the following:

- At least 2 hours of CE in medication safety/errors and

- At least 2 hours of CE in administering injectable

  medications, biological and adult immunizations if

  trained and are an authorized "Immunizing

  Pharmacist" and

- At least 2 hours of CE in the distribution, dispensing

  or delivery of controlled substances; or

- the detection and recognition of symptoms, patterns

  of behavior, or other characteristics of impairment and

  dependency resulting from the abusive or illegal use of

  controlled substances.

- For complete information on the CE

  requirements, see Section 1.4 and sections 14.1.3.1 of

  the Board's Rules and Regulations.

117

- Entering Continuing Education in the CE Tracker

- Continuing Education (CE) is tracked in <u>DELPROS</u>, the Delaware Professional Regulation Online Service. To enter your CE, you must first create a DELPROS user account. Go to the <u>DELPROS</u> online portal, and then click on Apply/Manage a License and Service Requests. If you are already an existing user, log in with your email address and password under the existing user section. have not yet created a DELPROS user account, click on REGISTER.

151.Answer: B

- Continuing Education Requirement

- The amount of continuing education (CE) that you are required to complete depends on when your license was issued during the full licensure period. If it is your first renewal, you are required to complete:

- 1.25 hours for each month between the initial date of licensure and the biennial renewal date

- Active Pharmacist licensees must complete 30 hours of approved CE during each full licensure renewal period between October 1 to September 30 even-numbered years (2020-2022, etc.) and must include the following:

- At least 2 hours of CE in medication safety/errors and

- At least 2 hours of CE in administering injectable medications, biological and adult immunizations if trained and are an authorized "Immunizing Pharmacist" and

- At least 2 hours of CE in the distribution, dispensing or delivery of controlled substances; or

- the detection and recognition of symptoms, patterns of behavior, or other characteristics of impairment and

119

dependency resulting from the abusive or illegal use of controlled substances.

- For complete information on the CE requirements, see Section 1.4 and sections 14.1.3.1 of the Board's Rules and Regulations.

- Entering Continuing Education in the CE Tracker

- Continuing Education (CE) is tracked in <u>DELPROS</u>, the Delaware Professional Regulation Online Service. To enter your CE, you must first create a DELPROS user account. Go to the <u>DELPROS</u> online portal, and then click on Apply/Manage a License and Service Requests. If you are already an existing user, log in with your email address and password under the existing user section. have not yet created a DELPROS user account, click on REGISTER.

152. Answer: B

- Continuing Education Requirement

- The amount of continuing education (CE) that you are required to complete depends on when your license was issued during the full licensure period. If it is your first renewal, you are required to complete:

- 1.25 hours for each month between the initial date of licensure and the biennial renewal date

- Active Pharmacist licensees must complete 30 hours of approved CE during each full licensure renewal period between October 1 to September 30 even-numbered years (2020-2022, etc.) and must include the following:

- At least 2 hours of CE in the area of medication safety/errors and

- At least 2 hours of CE in the area of administering injectable medications, biological and adult immunizations if trained and are an authorized "Immunizing Pharmacist" and

- At least 2 hours of CE in the distribution, dispensing or delivery of controlled substances; or

- the detection and recognition of symptoms, patterns of behavior, or other characteristics of impairment and dependency resulting from the abusive or illegal use of controlled substances.

- For complete information on the CE requirements, see Section 1.4 and sections 14.1.3.1 of the Board's Rules and Regulations.

- Entering Continuing Education in the CE Tracker

- Continuing Education (CE) is tracked in DELPROS, the Delaware Professional Regulation Online Service.

To enter your CE, you must first create a DELPROS

user account. Go to the DELPROS online portal, and

then click on Apply/Manage a License and Service

Requests. If you are already an existing user, log in

with your email address and password under the

existing user section. have not yet created a

DELPROS user account, click on REGISTER.

153.Answer: B

- Continuing Education Requirement

- The amount of continuing education (CE) that you are

  required to complete depends on when your license

  was issued during the full licensure period. If it is your

  first renewal, you are required to complete:

- 1.25 hours for each month between the initial date of

  licensure and the biennial renewal date

- Active Pharmacist licensees must complete 30 hours of approved CE during each full licensure renewal period between October 1 to September 30 even-numbered years (2020-2022, etc.) and must include the following:

- At least 2 hours of CE in the area of medication safety/errors and

- At least 2 hours of CE in the area of administering injectable medications, biological and adult immunizations if trained and are an authorized "Immunizing Pharmacist" and

- At least 2 hours of CE in the distribution, dispensing or delivery of controlled substances; or

- the detection and recognition of symptoms, patterns of behavior, or other characteristics of impairment and dependency resulting from the abusive or illegal use of controlled substances.

- For complete information on the CE requirements, see Section 1.4 and sections 14.1.3.1 of the Board's Rules and Regulations.

- Entering Continuing Education in the CE Tracker

- Continuing Education (CE) is tracked in <u>DELPROS</u>, the Delaware Professional Regulation Online Service. To enter your CE, you must first create a DELPROS user account. Go to the <u>DELPROS</u> online portal, and then click on Apply/Manage a License and Service Requests. If you are already an existing user, log in with your email address and password under the existing user section. have not yet created a DELPROS user account, click on REGISTER.

REFERENCES

1. Delaware Workers Cooperative Act, §§ 1401 to 1414

2. Delaware Revised Uniform Partnership Act, §§ 15-101 to 15-1210

3. Limited Partnerships, §§ 17-101 to 17-1208

4. Limited Liability Company Act, §§ 18-101 to 18-1208

5. Delaware Uniform Unincorporated Nonprofit Association Act, §§ 1901 to 1916

6. Certification of Adoption of Transparency and Sustainability Standards by Delaware Business Entities, §§ 5000E to 5008E

7. https://regulations.delaware.gov/AdminCode/title24/2500.shtml

8. DEA's Diversion Control Division Website www.DEAdiversion.usdoj.gov

9. DEA Homepage www.dea.gov

10. U.S. Government Publishing Office

11. https://www.govinfo.gov Provides access to the CFR, Parts 1300 to End, primary source for the Pharmacist's Manual, and the Federal Register which contains proposed and finalized amendments to the CFR.

12. Office of National Drug Control Policy (ONDCP)

    www.whitehouse.gov/ondcp

13. Food and Drug Administration www.FDA.gov

14. SAMHSA www.samhsa.gov

15. CSAT https://www.samhsa.gov/about-us/who-we-are/offices-centers/csat

16. Federation of State Medical Boards www.FSMB.org

17. National Association of Boards of Pharmacy

    https://nabp.pharmacy

18. National Association of State Controlled Substances

    Authorities **www.nascsa.org**

Made in the USA
Middletown, DE
03 February 2023

23889189R00076